The
GOOD
POET

22 23 24 25 26 7 6 5 4 3 2

ISBN: 979-8-9852433-5-2

Library of Congress Control Number: 2022910159

Editor: Kelly Lydick
Designer: Vanessa Mendozzi

PenTip Press
Jacksonville, FL
www.pentippress.com
www.kdgates.com

The GOOD POET

POETRY TO FEED, FORTIFY,
AND FULFILL THE SOUL

KD GATES

Contents

A Little Love Note

I still remember when she looked at me—hopelessness in her eyes—a fake smile on her face, and asked: "When did you know you were healed?" My answer: "I no longer gathered the broken pieces; that's when I knew I was whole." Some time has passed since then, and friends, my answer still stands. And the fortification of it lay rest on the pages of this book. My ups, downs, and in-betweens of all the good, bad, tragic, sad, and joyful moments that Life can bring peacefully slumber within The Good Poet— my heart's first cry. And to be honest, I've soaked many pillows. I've taken many directions, succumbed to plot twists, and packed for various destinations, hoping to go somewhere. But somewhere along the way, I stopped crying and started listening and learning. I stopped trying to map out life and embraced the road trip. And, here I am, an unintentional stoic going with the flow of Life. Riding waves, tasting the salt, all while understanding that there's nothing more remarkable in this life than knowing that you've gifted joy, peace, happiness, and hope to a life other than your own. If you yearn to heal and feel the joys of wholeness, I encourage you to release because sometimes, leaping requires letting go. After all, you can't stay still forever.

KD Gates

GOD

The hardest job you'll ever have is
convincing someone to believe
in a God they can't see.

If, in the end, there is no God,
then worry not. But, if in the end,
there turns out to be a God,
Hell has no fury like that.

The applause of man is

temporary.

The applause of God is

eternal.

A never fading,
glorious,
fruit-filled
applause.

To embody the Spirit of unity,

you must first embody the Spirit of Christ.

Oh Lord, align us, align us to fulfill
your will and not the pleasures
of our own disastrous desires.

Don't allow someone else to
determine your significance.
That's God's job.

When God created you,
He made you *good* and very *good*.
And, because He is significant,
that makes you significant
and *purposed* and *powerful*.

God
knows
you.

It's time that you know you.

If you don't know yourself,
how can you expect anyone else to know you?

A Family without God
is familiar destruction.

Chaos.

Calamity.

Confusion.

Catastrophe.

And Peace is nowhere to be found.

To be called an enemy
when God has placed you
as an ally and remain humble?

That's God!

That's strength, That's control,

That's Love.

To walk in God is to walk in
His confidence and His strength.

Not our own. Not our own.

Not our own. Not our own.

Not our own. Not our own.

Not our own. Not our own.

Not our own. Not our own.

We've tried every other way
and nothing.

Try *God* and gain a
whole lot of something.

Like peace of mind and growth,
and clarity and love and kindness.

Many are praising the
Universe yet failing to praise its Creator.

How does that work?

The storm belongs to God.
Let Him calm it.

P.S. He owns the rainbow, too.

God gives us choices.
The best choice we have is choosing

God's voice is not void or empty,
invalid, silent, or canceled.

However, the world wants us to believe that;
that God no longer speaks because if we can
ignore the King, we can hear the prince.

God has *never* failed me yet.
And, He never, ever, will.

GOD GAVE
US LIFE.

Use it to light up the world,
dark pathways and rooms,
schools, offices, unruly homes,
lukewarm churches, disobedient children,
atheists, satanist, and dim lighthouse
sitting atop the hill.

If you latch on to God and love yourself,
you will never seek validation from anyone else.

Seeking validation from others means
that we're unsure within.
Yet, we fail to realize that we seek approval from
other human beings, vessels with their problems,
demons, and battles to fight and, hopefully, win.
How can the insecure give security
or validation to anyone?

Again,

how can the insecure

give security or validation to anyone?

I love God's timing because His timing is perfect.
It's never an inconvenience to us,
although sometimes we may see it that way.
And, because we fail to respect His timing,
we miss blessings and are left wondering why
God hasn't answered prayers.

Moral of the story:
His timing. Not ours.

Your will.

My works.

Your wonders.

Miraculous results.

God whispers. The enemy shouts.

Hey enemy!

Why must you be so rude, belligerent,
and flighty to get my attention?
I mean— REALLY!

Reminder:

*God will
never tell you
to do anything
contrary to
who He is.*

I have stopped worrying about worrying about God!

Because,
if God does not have this, no man does.
And, if His hands can hold the whole world,
who am I to carry anything?

We can fall apart, break into a million pieces, and God will still put us back together again.

Whole.

Restored.

Revived.

Relieved.

Healed.

To repent is to turnaround.
It's asking what we can do for God
instead of asking what God can do for us.

If you don't believe in God and, in the end,
it turns out there is no God,
then you've lost nothing.

However, if you don't believe in God and in
the end, it turns out there is a God,
then you've lost **EVERYTHING**.

Do you really want to take that chance?

Man sees fault.
God sees favor.

Favor =
special benefits and
blessings granted to you.

Think about this, if generational curses, trauma, illness, and sins can travel from one generation to the next, so can strength, healing, love, power, and faith.
That's the kind of God that we serve!

Question:

Why do we easily allow the negatives to outweigh the positives in life?

LIFE

To become the monarch,
you must go through the metamorphosis of life.

The monarch: the icon of butterflies,
requires metamorphosis.
Our human lives are no different.
We don't go to sleep and wake up an icon
Life is a process of stages,
and it requires patience, strength, and tact.

We can't rush it. We can't skip it.
We must embrace it.

Embrace life as your own,

walking in its *essence*,

thriving to see its *excellence*.

Only then will you see your *excellence*.

Without chances, we minimize life,
opportunites, growth, success, and true happiness.

Without chances,
we minimize real change.

Your life.
Your responsibility.

Of course, staying down is easier
but getting up offers the sweetest rewards.

Who says you can't reconstruct your life?
Or start over?
Or dream big dreams?
Or try again and again and again
until you get it right?

You decide that.

You can't stay mad, sad,
and broken forever.
Life moves on and, if you're not careful,
it'll leave you behind.

Far, far behind.

Life, most of it, is hearsay because
society is too lazy to do the research.

P.S. Rumors spread faster than
dandelions in the spring.
However, unlike facts,
they can only run so far.

On the otherhand, facts

are seeds planted by the

mouth of the wise.

Expect blossoms.

What is life, if not created?

Your words have life—they can build a wall,
hold you captive, and leave you to rot.
However, speak the right words,
and they can tear it down—the wall,
your doubts, worries, anxieties, fears, and all.

ME

I've been hurt, rejected,
abandoned, molested, lied to, judged, taken
advantage of, scared, and hated.

But I've always been loved.

While they're worried about rivalry,
I'm running straight into purpose,
power, prosperity, wisdom, and blessings.

Head first!

I am a gift. My creation says so.

I am a gift. My creation says so.

I am a gift. My creation says so.

I am a gift. My creation says so.

I am a gift. My creation says so.

I am a gift. My creation says so.

I am a gift. My creation says so.

Molestation: that unseen,
yet very real monster under the bed.

*Last night, I kept my arms and feet tucked
tight in the bed. I wouldn't dare allow them
to hang over the edge. I was terrified of
the creepy monster under my bed.
Only, this time, he got me and left me for dead.*

If I'm going to fall in any direction,

it's not going to be backward or sideways.

**I'm falling forward and bringing
every good thing with me.**

Goodness works—
inside and outwardly.
Altruistic kindness grants
virtuous things.
In return, we receive
what we give out.

My pen is always ready.
Ready to write sweet notes, letter by letter,
line by line to you, the moon,
and afternoon showers at noon.

To vibrant vessels anxious to consume
the irrevocable, proverbial thoughts

I call *Mind*.

I may have cracks here and there.
But I refuse to be broken.

I refuse to be broken.

I refuse to be broken.

I refuse to be broken.

Find my voice? Well, was it lost?
Muted maybe, but *never* lost.

Growing up as a girl, I often heard people say,
"Find your voice," like it's playing hide-n-seek,
cat-and-mouse with me,
I'm the board—it's the game piece.
Clinching my lips, I often wanted to say:
"Go find your own voice and stop seeking mine."

But, with a lost voice, how could I?

I'm not crazy, and yes,

imperfections are necessary.

Our faults ingenuously enlighten

us to the idea that perfection

isn't real and that being

imperfectly perfect is.

You asked, "Why me?"
I answered, "Why not?"
Why not you?

-A love story

It's okay to be great, and the whole world knows it.

*I was that girl. Often minimizing my intelligence
to prevent offending the people in the room.
One day, a dear friend came to me and said,
"It's okay to be great, and the whole world knows it."
Those words hit differently. And I'm grateful.*

What I've learned

about bumps in the road,

is that you can step over them.

You may not like my answer.
But, today, my answer is no.

Tomorrow my answer may be no,
and the next day and the day after that, too.

Never be afraid to say "NO."

If I had to choose, to stand firm
on the bridge or to burn that b*tch down.
Oh, the choices we *must* make.

–Make wise choices

She turned pain into purpose,
dreams into reality, and,
as Selena so bravely said,

"Watch a girl!"

You asked me to do a good thing,
and "absolutely" was my answer.
I asked you to do an amazing thing,
and "complete silence" was yours.

*It doesn't matter how great you are,
how amazing your life may appear,
or what you have to offer. Sometimes,
people don't want to participate,
and we must be okay with that.*

We have to move on and live and laugh
and love, again and again and again.

INSPIRE

Inspiration:
the soul's indescribable love language.

To inspire is to love who you are while
responsibly sharing that love with everyone else.
So, aim to inspire whom
you can—where you can—when you can.

Magic isn't a mystery of witches or
a tale of fairies. It is extraordinary strength
resting within you.

The key, however,
is lifting the veil to see the magic.

Find your magic !

Can't find inspiration?

Prove to inspire yourself and have the heart
to share the wealth—inspiration that is.

Life's most significant wealth is
knowing that you've gifted joy, peace,
happiness, and hope to a life other than your own.

There's darkness, and there's light.
There's no in-between,
which means that we
have to make a choice:

Darkness or Light?

Bathe in confidence
and be your beautiful self.

Without regret.
Without doubt.
Without fear.
Just be confident.

It's the hidden figures that solve the puzzle.

"Men are from Mars; women are from Venus.
But I'm from somewhere different." I can account three
times in my life that I said those words to my mother.
As a girl, I felt different. I didn't fit in, and I felt alone.
My teenage years were no better.
Then, adulthood came, and that was the "awe ha"
moment! My feelings began to change,
and I started embracing my uniqueness.
I finally solved the puzzle—and I'm thrilled!
After all, why not be different?

CHANGE & POSITIVITY

To change for the better
feels uncomfortable.
But it's oh so necessary.

Fear is the emotional thing that we can't see.
We can feel it, but we can't see it.
Fear: the unseen keepsake
that keeps us from changing.

To create positive change,

you must be a positive change.

And to be a positive change,
one must want to change, challenge,
and compel the notion that
being unique is uncommon.

Be a sponge in a world of negativity
and soak up the positivity, vibrant life,
goodness, pure love,
and light this sphere has to give.

COURAGE

Have the courage to see and be something.

Courage isn't courage until employed. Once absorbed, allow it to drive you wild and conquer the "you know what" out of life!

P.S. Be fearless in the face of fear.

Have your own back while
having the *courage* to be yourself.

Being your authentic self takes *courage*,
and you will have naysayers,
haters, backstabbers, and doubters.
Keep going anyway.

Sometimes, leaping requires letting go.

Maya Angelou said,
"The caged bird sings,"
however, sometimes I think it shouts!

Feeling trapped is the suffocation of life,
and the yearning to escape is the lust.
Yet, if we find the courage to
nudge the cage, flying free is easy.

And soaring, even easier.

It takes courage to keep moving amid chaos,
amid unsupportive fake faces that yell

"I'm here" while deviously
whispering, "Sike."

This life takes courage.

Find the faith to embrace it.

JOY

If I had to choose between love and grief,
I openly, graciously, and selfishly choose joy!

To find joy in a world painted with sorrow is
the pot of gold at the end of the rainbow.
When you find it,
bind it around your heart
and keep it there!

Share a little, too.

**Joy is the greater
side of sorrow,
just as smiling is the
greater side of frowning.**

Joy is choosing Jesus over self while being
completely happy with the choice.

I'm not shy when I say that

I'm a Christian.

Honestly, I've never been happier.

LOVE

For surely,
it's not a head thing.
It's a heart thing.

The world confuses love with avoidance,
keeping it under lock and key.
But once you've felt authentic love,
you no longer bond to what the world thinks,
you bond to what your heart speaks.
Love is very real, and it's not in your head.

When you find it, you will know it.

Help is to love as hinder is to hate.

Listening to ambitious words is feeling the desire without proof. Instead, allow actions to dictate the response and decide accordingly—are you here to help me, or are you here to hurt me?

Because when you love someone, you support them.

Love hard because love is and
will always be the answer.

Side Notes:

Never, ever loose yourself to love.
Love and lust are different.
Physical, mental,
emotional abuse is not love.

A grateful heart is a magical heart.

Who says you can't create magic,
call it confetti, and sprinkle it everywhere?

Love doesn't merely grow; it evolves,
making it Earth's most significant asset.
And the gains; great. Honestly,
it's never too late to teach it,
feel it, or learn it.

Christianity isn't a chore.
It's a love, a way of life where
the monetary
reward is insignificant,
and the gains of peace gifted.

FAITH

It takes faith and boldness to make moves and to keep moving.

Faith, often called the "mustard seed" theory, is hope. It's having confidence in the unseen things that you hoped for and the assurance that those things are coming forth. Honestly, we all hope. Where would we be without it?

Faith is the foundation.

Without faith we stumble
and tumble and crumble
until we all fall down.

To wish upon a star is merely 50 percent of the process.
I'd rather put my trust in the star's *Creator* and gain the whole 100.

P.S. If given a choice between 50% of a maybe and 100% of surety,

always choose the latter.

Worry sees the problem. Faith sees the solution.

Instead of asking for social stats
and phone numbers, ask them about their faith.

Many broken hearts would cease
to break if initially,
instead of asking for social handles,
we asked about faith.

Do you believe in God?
Do you love Him?
Do you have faith?
Do you love yourself?

The faith of *God*
takes away
the fear of man.

It's through our faith that
we're able to see through our fears,
conquer anxieties, and *live*.

Let the wind waver, not your faith.

Let the wind waver, not your faith.

Let the wind waver, not your faith.

Let the wind waver, not your faith.

Faith saves the day!

At least if you believe.

BELIEVE

To believe in the impossible
is to believe in the King.

In other words,
Limiting who you are and what you can do,
limits God and what He can do.
And, there's nothing that He can't do.

Stop waiting for others to believe in you and believe in yourself.

If you're waiting for others to believe in you,
you're going to be waiting forever.
Instead, believe in yourself first,
and others will follow.

We're endless lights of
possibility when we believe.

To mentally touch you is to consciously see you.
And, if I can see you, then
I can better you—and you can better him,
and he can better her, and she can better them.
Belief is a three-strand chord not easily broken.

Fearlessly believe in the true *King*.
Believe and believe hard, even if it kills you.

The rebirth is worth it!

PRAYER

Prayer is finding balance between
self and soul while knowing that God is in control.

Prayer doesn't prevent failure.
It gives you the strength to get up again,
again, and again until you make it.

Until you push through.
Until you overcome.
Until you believe.
Utill you release the
idea that you're in control.

Give gifts of peace and prayer,
for both are priceless and
yield irreplaceable rewards.

Fear is to darkness as light is to prayer.
So, if you're going to cease anything,
cease fear.

The church, through prayer and faith, controls the land.

P.S. Watered down is a term for plants, not Christians.

HEALING

When things fester and die within us,

we become those things; we become *bound*.

And bondage is a self-inflicted *wound*.

Healing, therefore, becomes a requirement,

allowing opportune tranquility to

overtake chaos and drama.

You don't have to kill someone physically to "kill" them. If you can capture a person spiritually and mentally, then you have them. Don't allow anyone to kill you.

You're the CEO of your mind.

Rejection

Rejection indeed is a blessing.
It's God's divine protection over your life.

i.e. a timewaster. A person walking
Waste of Time Lane and circling Dead End Loop.

Things left untreated
are repeated.

You can either live with
the burden or clear it—your choice.

Let the past be past tense.

To be balanced spiritually, mentally,
and physically is to be beautiful.

Restoration is the fortification
we inhabit to resist those sticks and stones.

No broken bones here.

Words hurt. But, the majority of verbal abuse
is a person's way of regurgitating their self-reflection
onto others. In other words, it's not about you;
it's about them.

WOMEN

As women, we're not only beautiful;
we're magnificently brilliant.
And, that's a bold something to be.

Once we as women defy the social norms
of being beauty queens
and understand that we're giants,
our flames would be eternal.

#SheGiant

The Wolf

You took life and threw me away—
in a fit of rage, setting my stage,
as I became the wildfire and
you started the blaze.
Thank you.

*Ladies hear me! You will drown
in your tears for years until
you understand this: you unknowingly
met the wolf when you were used
to herding the sheep.*

*Translation: Wolf in sheeps clothing
or a seemingly kind man with bad intentions.*

It's the weak and insecure minds that compete rather than collaborate.

An insecure woman will create a competition
that you know nothing about.
And, when you win, cry wolf.

This world is living, and if you see
yourself as no good, the world too,
will treat you and see you as no good.

*Ladies, the way you treat yourself
is the way the world will treat you.*

It takes tough skin to stride
in the shoes she's in. Still, want them?

Translation: A jealous woman favors vanity
and fails to see pure hearts. Yet, a modest woman
seeks to know the character and the
content traveling with it.

Are you allowing withdrawals without deposits? Ladies, check your balance.

Would you open a bank account,
fill it with your life's savings, and give all the
funds to a stranger? Probably not.
Then why would you do that with
your heart and soul—your internal life savings?
Think about that question before giving
the goodness of who you are to ungrateful people.

Bragging: another way of screaming
for the attention you aren't getting.

Momma, unlike Forest, never said,

"Life was like a box
of chocolates."

Instead, they're somewhat bitter or sweet, she says.
But the creamy one in the box is unique—
the one you need to be. Be her, and you will
never seek attention; instead,
attention will seek you.

You're a go-getter. So be a go-getter and go get it!

Love, what's stopping you?

Ladies, surround yourself with people willing to water you during the drought.

As women, we often hold on to people for far too long hoping for a positive change. That change usually never comes requiring us to make the ultimate decision, keep them or release them?

My advice: If fake friends, family members, or companions refuse to water you, CUT THEM LOSE! Because at the end of the day, you can be dry all by yourself.

Would it be so sexist to say that it's the
"*she*" in me that makes me resilient?

Oh, how powerful women are.
When I think about it,
we're downright miraculous.
Jesus fortified our strength when
He first revealed Himself and the news
about His resurrection to a woman.
Mary Magdalene was her name,
and she, too, was resilient.

Why not shine at the same time and share the light?

Indeed, if insecurity, jealousy, envy,
or fear isn't the problem,
what's wrong with sharing
the lime or the light?

STRENGTH

Your strength surpasses you. Don't let anyone take it.

Have the strength and confidence to say yes,
the guts to follow through,
and the tenacity to let go.

To give your strength to another
human being is an indication that
it's not weakness
that you're battling;
it's your mind and the hurt it carries.
Let go.

A man's emotions aren't a sign of weakness.
It's a sign of strength and vulnerability.
And that itself is super.
Honestly, every woman on Earth
would forgo *Clark Kent for the Real Deal.

*Super Man

To say "no" and mean it is the brave girl's definition of strength.

No is a two-letter word, yet one of the most
challenging words to confidently say.
Yet, if you find the strength to utter it,
you'll experience newfound freedom,
growth, confidence, and resilience.

And, when the time is right to say "yes,"
have the strength and confidence to say it,
the guts to follow through, and the tenacity
to let go of it when it's time to say "no" again.

You only stay because you lack the guts to go.

The fear of the unknown leaves us
to die in hellacious situations.
But, woe to the warrior within you!
Once you find the heart to go,
you'll ask yourself why it took so long.

It takes strong bones to remain alone.
Especially when they think
you're following the crowd.

Cliques are and always will be
insecure souls afraid of

Loneliness and Different.

FORGIVENESS

There's no red, green, or blue pill
for forgiveness, no quick fix
Forgiveness takes learning to
lean on the source while taking life
one day at a time.

The art of apologizing
is very relevant.
It's a prerequisite
to forgiveness.

*Forgiveness is
the real soul food.*

Ingestion of life is an inevitable lesson
and people will eat bits and pieces of you
until they swallow you whole.
However, It's how you digest the
teaching that matters.

In other words, eat the meat
and spit out the bones.

To be good to someone who wasn't

good to you is not only grace; it's *compassion*

and the ability to experience boundless,

unlimited, *unconditional love*.

SELF / LOVE

Self-love is real love because
if you love yourself, you can recognize
and accept real love from someone else.

You are what you think.
Love yourself and the world will know it.
Hate yourself and the world
will know that too—your choice.

Self-doubt
is an inside job.

P.S. Firing the insubordinate
employee is always an option.

To be authentically great at anything requires
an authentic love of self. And, a love of
self grants a genuine opportunity to
believe and achieve great things.

Praise yourself and believe that it's good.

Note:

Believe that you are worthy of celebration,
and don't ever be afraid to pat yourself
on the back—to celebrate your wins, big or small.
Celebrate them all.

Don't dim your light for someone else's gain.

If they love you, they will bask in the glow.

A nobody to self.
A somebody to someone else.

*I've always said that people say and do things
all the time. However, it's not what they say;
it's about what you say, how you feel about yourself,
and the desire to utilize the life you've been gifted.
Because life itself is epic, it offers grand rewards,
and you are worthy of them all. The key is believing
that you are worthy.*

People go, people, stay.
But *"alleluia!"* to those who stay,
please stay forever.

Rejection is the blessing you never knew you needed.

Love yourself enough to do what's right for you, even if it hurts.

To know better and to do better,
lets us realize that we deserve better.
Much, much better.

MISERY

Misery usually has company. Often, that company is us.

The key, however, is to stop having affairs with Misery, destined loneliness.

Often, we're comfortable in pain, fearful of letting go, and terrified of the unknown. Yet, if we release, we heal, and Joy becomes the company we keep.

PURPOSE

Created on purpose, with purpose,

for a specific purpose.

To be here without purpose would be a waste
of time on God's part, and that,
my friend, is not possible.
God does everything on purpose,
including creating you– on purpose,
with a specific purpose, and for a specific purpose.

To be brave enough is the willingness
to embrace the unknown. To confront the
insecurities behind the door.
To be brave is to be passionate about
purpose and to kiss the
you know what out of it.

Channel
your
inner
brave!

Definite purpose
is a promise.
Finding it,
understanding it,
and embracing
it is the challenge.

Destiny is direction, guides,
and connections with one purpose: to
guide the lost to their purpose
while connecting us all back to Him.

The Creator.

DOUBT

Seeds of doubt may be planted. However, they can only grow when watered.

People will doubt you,
that's just the way the cookie crumbles.
However, it's not up to them; it's up to you—
seeds of doubt sprout when you water them.

Doubt is easier, although it offers the least rewards.

Belief is challenging,
yet it offers great rewards.

Woe! to the man who doubts himself—

your journey ahead will be lengthy

with many winding roads and plot twists.

Make sure to pack light;

you'll be in the *wilderness* for a while.

FRIENDSHIP

Sometimes, the snake sits at the table with you. But so does the eagle.

Remember to keep your eyes open,
true friends want you to win,
and being a snake is far too ordinary,
opt to be the eagle instead.

Not all friendships are painful,
nor are they perfect.
But, a friend that continually hurts you
is not a friend at all and, in the end,
will eventually betray you.

Friends have two faces: those
that graciously esteem you and
those that carefully undermine you.

BUT

Real friends are triple threats.
They refresh the mind, body, and soul.

Choose wisely.

Lost pieces can be
found in a good friend.

PEACE

Peace is the conductor of the orchestra. Joy, happiness, and hope are the instruments.

Yes,

peace is an inside job.

But peace, like rhythm,
can be quiet or loud;
ultimately, it's all about perception.

Peace:
the epitome
of a permanent
vacation.

PAIN

Pain is NOT mandatory.

*We have the choice to sit in mental
anguish or to let it go.
Because pain, unlike love,
is never mandatory unless we allow it to be.*

Will you release inner turmoil for peace?

Shame, the hidden side of pain,

will dilute your most remarkable

characteristics, mute your *talents*,

silence your *capabilities*, and destroy

viable *opportunities* every time.

Pain isn't permanent.
It becomes persistent when we allow
it to become familiar.

friendly.

family.

facts.

fear.

Sometimes, the trash of life takes itself out.
And, we must be ever so thankful for that.

People come, and people go.
Don't drown, wallow, or sit in the pain of them
walking away.
Make the pain matter,
and become your best self.

You can't move into your future chained
to your past. So leave the hurt, take the lesson,
and understand that the pain won't always last.

Let the pain go
and grow.

GROWTH

Yes, growth is a process,
and with it comes grudges.
But, it's the completion of the
climb that wins the gold.

We stop growing when we limit ourselves.

I don't recall seeing the word
"limit" etched on foreheads or hearts,
so stop limiting yourself and start flourishing,
producing, and building brilliant things.

Why do good when you have innumerable
opportunities to do great?

Do the best you can with what you have until you can do better. Then, do your best.

There's always a Judas at the table. After all, without him, there's no growth.

But, be careful; most often, those we label Judas may be John, and those we call James may be Judas.

BLESSINGS

Blessings
are spiritual healers.
They're refreshing.
Allow them to
medicate you.

Like anything in life, the refreshing takes time,
and chasing dragons will not decrease the wait.
So, rather than seeking a quick fix, respect "right now"
blessings while understanding that our gifts
don't abandon us; we reject them.

People miss out on blessings every day;
praise God that you weren't one of those people.
But, if you were one of those people,
remember that blessings, like hands on a clock,
have a beautiful way of coming back around.
Only this time, don't miss the blessing.

ANGER

When Anger speaks
it's likely wrong.
Therefore, instead of
criticizing, teach.
Instead of
getting angry, talk.

Rage! Pick it up, put it down.
Pick it up, put it down.
Oh, rage!
The struggle is real.

—**Anger**

Change the world by
changing your words
and habits and thoughts
and ideas and tone.

A foolish man is often angry and unwise.

Once you get over the offense,
I pray that you accept the lesson.

There's a lesson
in all things.

CHARACTER

Don't take it with a grain of salt. Take the whole saltshaker!

Real character shows through behavior.
Sadly, we often overlook the caution
lights and stop signs.
Next time, instead of believing in mere
maybes and ifs, believe in hard truths,
character, and content.

To act without thought derogates character every time.

People are people. Period!

Four of the most powerful words ever.
In other words, never allow people to
shock you; they're unpredictable.

Momma taught me that. Thanks, Mom!

Greater
not greater than.

The goal is to know greater and embrace your
version of it, knowing that you are not better
than anyone else. Yet, worthy of greatness.

If the good presents itself,
always strive for the extraordinary.

Because, who
you are today,
tomorrow,
and forever is
entirely up to
YOU.

Secret dislike is only secret to the person
secretly thinking the other person
doesn't know the secret.
Confidentially, friction is a feeling,
and it made an entrance long
before your hello ever did.

Make your bed, lie in it.
Now, make it again, and this time, do it neatly.

Moral of the story:

Life is a set of choices,

mistakes are lessons,

and the final grade depends on

how well you studied for the test.

*People will merely
paint their picture of you.
It's up to you to
paint the masterpiece.*

**Don't allow others to paint your story;
after all, people paint messy pictures.
Have the guts to pick up the brush and
paint the very best portrait of yourself.**

SUCCESS

Falling isn't the tragedy.
Refusing to get up
is the tragedy.

To the girl that fell often, thank you for getting up!
What I learned is that success requires falling,
stumbling, and sliding.
After all, failure ensues when you refuse to get up.
So, get up, brush yourself off, and keep moving.

Because you only fail when you stop trying.

Make exceptional waves
and ride them.
Taste the salt,
feel the sun,
and when done,
swim with success.

Yesterday I did.

Today I do.

Tomorrow I will.

Success—my infinite ability,

and I will embrace

every present moment.

Run for it, you can't stay still forever.
Your destiny waits at I'm A Success Lane,
and Yes I Won't Quit Avenue.

And, if you get lost along the way,
GPS (Go Past Stagnant) and find your way back.

Because there is nothing
to it but to do it.

However, let it be done in season—boldly, confidently, and gracefully.

After all, why dream-a-dream
if all you do is dream it?

xo Success

To jump off the cliff or sit on the ledge, that's the question you need to answer.

......

The experiences of life are brutal
companions destined to
lead us to the cliff.
Jumping off,
however, is the decision.
We can allow the pains of life
to conquer us, or we can defeat them.
The choice is ours.

A NOTE ABOUT THE AUTHOR

She's the visionary behind the smile and the woman who almost became a Nun—twice.

K.D. Gates, a lover of well-written words, garnered a strong love for poetry at a young age. Reading classics by Maya Angelou, Hellen Keller, and Mark Twain, gave her a deep appreciation for inspirational quotes and healing notes.

Seeking to enhance her educational expertise, K.D. obtained a bachelor's degree in Business Management, and following, through entrepreneurship, became a featured expert on Essence.com and Today.com.

Later, after reflecting on her adolescent years of childhood trauma, parental rejection, and fear, K.D., noticed she found a sense of release and contentment through writing, dreaming, and learning—three of her best-loved hobbies.

Now, the woman behind the smile, K.D., continues to compose quotes and short notes to impact, heal, and inspire others.

A Florida native for over forty years, K.D., enjoys spending time with family, reading, laughing with friends, solving mysteries, and writing.

DEDICATION

Her character, strength, and resilience built me.
Her tenacity, love, and peaceful demeanor fortified
me. And her enduring faith, well, that made me
unstoppable. As Abraham Lincoln so graciously
stated, "All I am or hope to be, I owe to my mother."
Like Abraham, all that I am and all that I hope to
be, I owe to my mother. Barbara, I love you.

AFTERWORD

Two worlds collided and, in the blink of an eye, became the perfect match.

In her book, The Good Poet, a collection of intimate quotes and notes, K.D. combines natural and spiritual sentiments to heal, inspire, and transform the minds of her readers. Deemed an extraordinary symmetry of strength and courage, The Good Poet is a life-changing, remarkable treasure to love.

ACKNOWLEDGMENTS

I had a dream that seemed far yonder. Yet, you gazed and saw magnificent wonders. Dream pushers, believers, risk-taking achievers, you dared to stare, and for that, I'm eternally grateful. Jermaine Ross, Sylvia Miller-Howell, and friends, You Rock!